IMAGES
of America

BIG BEND
NATIONAL PARK
AND VICINITY

ON THE COVER: Boquillas del Carmen, on the "Old Mexico" side of the Rio Grande, is the gateway to an International Peace Park, proposed in 1936, joining Big Bend and Mexico. In 1959, when Jack Boucher took this photograph, he probably never dreamed it would one day be impossible for park visitors to freely cross over and experience the ambience of frontier Mexico or walk in the fir and pine forest on the Fronteriza range. Perhaps someday the idea of an international park will once again become reality. (Courtesy of the U.S. National Park Service.)

IMAGES
of America

BIG BEND
NATIONAL PARK
AND VICINITY

Thomas C. Alex

ARCADIA
PUBLISHING

Copyright © 2010 by Thomas C. Alex
ISBN 978-0-7385-7853-8

Published by Arcadia Publishing
Charleston, South Carolina

Printed in the United States of America

Library of Congress Control Number: 2009928045

For all general information contact Arcadia Publishing at:
Telephone 843-853-2070
Fax 843-853-0044
E-mail sales@arcadiapublishing.com
For customer service and orders:
Toll-Free 1-888-313-2665

Visit us on the Internet at www.arcadiapublishing.com

*To the explorers and determined settlers who spent time
in Big Bend and recorded their experiences.*

CONTENTS

ACKNOWLEDGMENTS

This publication is a simple introduction that hopefully inspires the reader to seek a much deeper and profoundly detailed history of one of the nation's crown jewels, Big Bend National Park. Far more information lies waiting to be revealed than could be encompassed in a publication of this size. Archival sources of images and information include Huntington Library in San Marino, California; archives of the Big Bend, Bryan Wildenthal Library at Sul Ross State University in Alpine, Texas; Museum of the Big Bend at Sul Ross State University; Big Bend National Park photographic archives; National Park Service Historic American Engineering Record; and Marfa and Presidio County Museum in Marfa, Texas. Thanks go to those who have donated historical information to these archives. Special acknowledgment goes to Dr. Ross Maxwell, Nellie Rice, Patricia Wilson Clothier, Julia Nail Moss, Bobby Wilson, María Zamarron Bermudez, Sr. and Alejandro and Sra. Estefana Sandate, Martín Sandate for his assistance, John Morlock, Cynta de Narvaez, Jack Burgess, Bob Wirt, John Alexander, Ringo Smith, Jim and Carolyn Burr, Barbara Trammell, Terlingua Fire and Emergency Services, National Parks Concessions Inc., Brewster County Historical Commission, Texas Archeological Society, and Arcadia's Kristie Kelley for her encouragement and patience. A special tribute goes to Betty Alex for enduring the struggle to compile this work and for her dedicated editing to keep the whole thing in line, including its author's rambling verbosity. The utmost tribute goes to those people who recognize the value in preserving their family history and preserving their family photographs by donating them to archival institutions for the benefit of all.

INTRODUCTION

The Big Bend, as it is called today, is a most unique and diverse landscape, and the role humankind has played is equally diverse. The visual impression may be both inspiring and disturbing. Many who come to Big Bend have difficulty accepting the seemingly harsh face of the desert with its thorny scrub brush, cactus, and apparent desolation. But those seeking deeply with their inner being can begin to touch the occult mystery of the desert that slowly unfolds like a blossom on a prickly pear. Therein lies a depth unique in the world, and those who are fortunate enough to glimpse its magic are truly blessed.

Although the first Europeans on the scene considered the land *el despoblado*, or "the uninhabited land," humans have lived here for millennia and referred to themselves in their own tongues as simply *the people*. But over 10,000 years ago the face of this landscape appeared far different than today. In those latter days of the last great ice age, a cooler climate brought two rainy seasons. Winter rains brought forth a rich diversity of plant life in the spring—a broad blanket of grasses, populated with juniper, oak, and pine trees extending from the peaks of the Chisos Mountains to the Rio Grande. Dry arroyos today were once streams flowing with water for long periods, lined with thickets of oak, juniper, hackberry, Mexican persimmon, and other fruit-bearing species. The summer rainy season replenished the earth with moisture, sustaining the rich blanket of vegetation through the heat of the year. The people were able to camp most anywhere and find abundant wild plants and a wide array of animals, both of which they relied upon for food, clothing, and shelter.

Then for 10 millennia, the desert slowly overtook this landscape, winter monsoons diminished, and summer monsoons supported fewer woodland species at lower elevations. Desertification migrated slowly to the foot of the Chisos Mountains and the lower elevations transformed with an array of diverse desert succulents, shrubs, and grasses. During this time, people learned which of these could provide nutrition, medicine, and other tools of survival. Intimate knowledge of the landscape equated to survival of the people.

Spanish explorers traveled into these northern territories and encountered bands of Chizo Indians, part of a larger group of Conchos Indians, who fiercely resisted Spanish settlement. Europeans brought horses, metal tools, and weapons, and they forcibly imposed Old World religious views upon the ancient cultural patterns of the people. Horses provided them with greater mobility, allowed territorial expansion, and facilitated warfare against traditional adversaries. Settlements by white-skinned strangers with their new technologies also brought diseases, a new social order, and land-altering agricultural practices. A desire for these new technologies drove American Indians to wage warfare far beyond their traditional range. Plains Indians annually passed through the Big Bend, striking deeply into Spanish territory, taking livestock, capturing slaves, and causing fear among European settlers. By around 1700, Mescalero and Lipan Apache displaced the Chizo, but these nomadic invaders only sporadically occupied the land. The Comanche made annual forays through the area to plundering grounds as far south as the state of Durango, 500 miles into Mexico.

During the 18th century, the Spanish government established military fortresses, or presidios, to bring order to Nueva Vizcaya (New Spain). For a short time (1775–1784), Spanish soldiers staffed presidios at San Carlos and San Vicente on the south side of the Rio Grande. The Spanish soon abandoned these forts because of inefficiency at deterring invaders, financial burdens on the government, and extreme difficulty of resupply and communications with such remote locations.

After the war between the United States and Mexico (1846–1848), under the Treaty of Guadalupe Hidalgo, Big Bend became part of the United States of America. Anglo Americans attempting to settle the frontier encountered hostilities from American Indians who still claimed the land. After 1850, American military expeditions began systematically mapping the area's geography and inventorying its resources.

In 1854, Fort Davis (130 miles north of park headquarters) was established along the San Antonio–El Paso Road to protect travelers and frontier settlers. Fort Stockton was established in 1859 at Comanche Springs, a major water stop at the intersection of the famous Comanche War Trail, the Butterfield Overland Mail Route, and the San Antonio-Chihuahua freight road. In the 1880s, the army established Camp Peña Colorado and Camp Neville Springs along the Comanche Trail as outposts of Fort Clark, and troops of the 10th Cavalry, known as "Buffalo Soldiers," garrisoned these frontier forts.

The first ranchers entering the area found what appeared to be lush and abundant grazing land, but once ranches were established, settlers realized the tenuous hold they possessed on this sometimes unforgiving desert. The G4 Ranch, established in 1885, was one of the largest in the Trans-Pecos. By 1895, drought and other problems forced closure and subdivision of the ranch. Other large ranches, like the Buttrill Ranch in the north Rosillos Mountains, encountered similar problems in the early 20th century. Numerous families tried to make a living but found the desert unyielding. Others met success through ingenuity and perseverance.

Around 1895, several mineral discoveries brought another economy to the area. From northern Mexico, the Puerto Rico Mine brought lead, zinc, and silver ore into the United States via a 6-mile aerial tramway. Other mines at Mariscal Mountain and in the Terlingua Mining District produced mercury from cinnabar ore in quantities rivaling the famous Almaden Mine in Spain.

These enterprises spurred the growth of communities and attracted people seeking escape from the turmoil of the Mexican Revolution and a better life for their families. Between 1916 and 1920, political strife in Mexico made it easy for bandits to take advantage of the political confusion to plunder local settlements. Some settlers found it easier to leave than persevere in a vast landscape having very little law enforcement. But in general, military encampments established to protect the locals found very little hostile activity. Prior to September 11, those in law enforcement found the area particularly uneventful.

Two world wars, the Great Depression, and the growing urbanization of the 20th century created a national need for places where Americans could escape and find recreational opportunities. The lands that were set aside and placed under the management of the U.S. National Park Service have become the refuges where Americans can go when times are good or bad and seek personal renewal. The Buffalo Soldier motto "We Can, We Will" testifies to the determination of all those who strove to find a home in this remote and wild frontier. Some found success, some experienced failure, and some realized that even though they had to leave, they found their souls possessed by the spirit that is the Big Bend. Americans today can come to the park and in the solitude, the quiet, and the immense expanse of the creation, find their personal ties to the universe.

This work is neither comprehensive nor detailed but presents the reader with snapshots of a place with unfathomable depth. It offers a selection of uncommon images of places and people, and the book suggests alternative views not previously expressed by other authors.

One

THE FIRST PEOPLE

No one knows what the first Americans called themselves. Most indigenous groups referred to themselves in their own language as *the people* in the same way they referred to *the animals, the sky, the earth,* and *the creator.* Some tribes referred to other groups by the name of that group's leader.

In the 1600s, Spanish priests established the first missions at agricultural villages at La Junta, the confluence of the Rio Conchos and Rio Grande, near modern-day Ojinaga, Chihuahua, Mexico, and Presidio, Texas. The Catholic priests learned the native tongues so they could convert and instruct the American Indian in Christian ways. When asking about neighboring tribes, the people of La Junta called the ones living in the present-day national park Chizo. According to scholar T. N. Campbell, the name Chizo originally referred to one band also known as Cacuitaome or Taquitatome. The Spaniards extended the Chizo to include at least six closely associated bands that were culturally related to Uto-Aztecan people of northern Mexico.

By the early 1800s, Spanish occupation of this territory consisted of small settlements called *rancherias* centered on ranching and farming. Most settlements were located at reliable springs or along permanent streams. Spanish horses gave the native people greater mobility, enabling groups from the southern plains to drive deeply into Spanish territory seeking additional riding stock and weapons that they often took with impunity. The settlements just south of the Rio Grande fought, fled, or made pacts with these invaders. The Chizo were displaced by northern tribes, and some accounts place the scattered remnants of Chizo with their cultural kindred in Mexico where they absorbed that group's identity. Eventually Europeans overcame the native people and irreversibly imprinted the landscape.

History is defined when someone inscribes a meaningful record, which survives the ravages of time, as seen above. Languages live and die with the cultures that use them, and the meaning the petroglyphs held for the person who etched them are lost to time. Prehistoric people used natural shelter and ingenuity to protect themselves from adverse weather and climate. Below, this *jacal*-type (pronounced Ha-Kal) construction evolved from methods used by prehistoric people throughout the southwest United States—a framework of poles and sticks was plastered with mud to seal against wind and rain. Under the recess of this rock overhang that provides a natural roof is a combination of jacal and rock enclosing the living space. An external jacal provides additional shelter and storage space. (Above photograph by author; below photograph by George Grant, courtesy of U.S. National Park Service.)

In the 1600s, Spanish explorers recorded Jumano Indians at numerous locations across Texas and New Mexico. Jumano traders obtained turquoise and textiles from pueblos, such as Taos Pueblo along the northern reach of the Rio Grande, and secured buffalo hides from the southern plains, trading these items along their routes through northeast and central Texas and westward to El Paso. Priests at La Junta de los Rios (modern-day Presidio, Texas) mentioned that Jumano traded with permanent agricultural villages in the area. Scholars working in the area suspect that the Jumano assimilated into the Apache. (Courtesy of U.S. National Archives and Records Administration, Record Group 106, Smithsonian Institution, Bureau of American Ethnology.)

During the 1700s, tension arose between Spanish and native people who held vastly diverse views and practiced drastically different lifestyles. Apaches raided Spanish settlements and then fled, seeking refuge in the intensely rugged mountains of Big Bend and northern Mexico. The Chizo Indians, their native range centered on the Chisos Mountains, fled these invaders to the protection of cultural kindred in northern Mexico. (Courtesy of U.S. National Archives and Records Administration, Record Group 111, U.S. Department of the Army, Office of the Chief Signal Officer.)

11

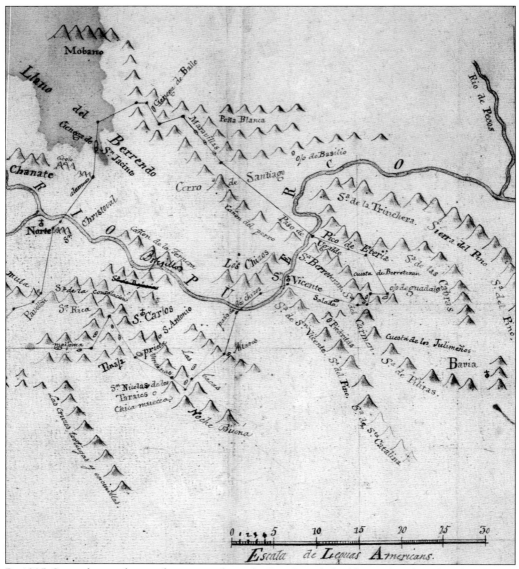

By 1805, Spanish presidios, or fortresses, along the Rio Grande had been abandoned and no longer protected the settlements of San Carlos, San Antonio, Altarez, Piedritas, and Salada south of the Rio Grande. Native American raiders from the north frequently plundered Spanish settlements, capturing fresh riding stock and occasionally taking slaves. At San Carlos, people made pacts with invaders to secure their existence in this remote frontier. In many Spanish settlements like San Carlos, Europeans intermarried with native people, creating a rich intercultural mingling of Old World and New World knowledge and traditions. This combined ancient knowledge with unique practical wisdom, enabling their survival in an otherwise hostile environment. This wisdom forms a significant part of the heritage of today's Hispanic people. (Map reproduced by permission of the Huntington Library, San Marino, California.)

In the 1800s, settlers moving westward in search of homesteads and economic opportunities were met by the original landholders—Comanche, Kiowa, and Plains Apache Indians. These native people resisted encroachment and frequently found themselves in fierce battle to protect their homeland. (Courtesy of National Archives and Records Administration, Record Group 106, Smithsonian Institution, Bureau of American Ethnology.)

Inevitably it became obvious that reconciliation and peace were necessary. Despite fierce resistance from within, Indian representatives attempted to reach a lasting peace between both groups. Peace treaties are only as good as the parties' willingness to abide by them, and the whites notoriously failed to honor treaties. Groups with widely divergent views rarely find complete agreement and such is the history of relations between Indian Nations and the U.S. government. (Courtesy of National Archives and Records Administration, Record Group 106, Smithsonian Institution, Bureau of American Ethnology.)

Entrance to Cañon of San Carlos, Rio Bravo del Norte.

After the Treaty of Guadalupe Hidalgo in 1848, the land north of the Rio Grande became U.S. territory, and Anglo expeditions into the region attempted to ascertain what lay in this unknown frontier. Maj. William H. Emory, chief astronomer and surveyor of the U.S. Boundary Commission, and M. T. W. Chandler passed through the area in December 1852. As they surveyed the Rio Grande, the expedition crossed numerous ancient Indian trails, and at Comanche Pass (today's Lajitas, Texas), the survey party encountered a Comanche band crossing the Rio Grande towards Durango, Mexico. Chandler proposed the name of Mount Emory for the highest visible peak that the survey party used for triangulation measurements for miles along their route. (Courtesy of Maj. William H. Emory's Report of the United States and Mexican Boundary Survey, Volume I, 1857, Big Bend National Park Archives.)

Mount Emory—Los Chisos mountains – Rio Bravo del Norte.

The most striking account was written by M. T. W. Chandler during the expedition, "It proved to be a country cut up with deep arroyos, presenting to the survey almost insurmountable obstacles. Passing these arroyos, a wild valley, nearly at right angles with the course of the river, preceded the approach to the cañon of Sierra Carmel [the name used in the 1800s for Sierra del Carmen], another of those rocky dungeons in which the Rio Grande is for a time imprisoned. No description can give an idea of the grandeur of the scenery through these mountains. There is no verdure to soften the bare and rugged view; no overhanging trees or green bushes to vary the scene from one of perfect desolation." (Courtesy of Maj. William H. Emory's Report of the United States and Mexican Boundary Survey, Volume I, 1857, Big Bend National Park Archives.)

Apache, Comanche, and Kiowa Indians shared sparsely scattered springs along the Comanche Trail. Between 1879 and 1893, several detachments of U.S. Infantry and Cavalry occupied military encampments, providing protection for travelers and settlers. South of Grapevine Hills, Neville Spring's flowing water and trees served as home during the 1880s for a group of Buffalo Soldiers, an outpost of Fort Clarks' 10th Cavalry. (Courtesy of Museum of the Big Bend.)

Long before the Spanish arrived and settled at San Carlos, American Indians camped there because of the abundant water. During the Comanche and Kiowa raiding period, settlers at San Carlos made pacts with American Indians who maintained peaceful encampments at the village. On the left is Balentin Chavez, born at San Carlos in 1860, and on the right is Santiago Lujan. Their parents were also born at San Carlos in the early 1800s. These *viejos*, or old men, relayed accounts of American Indian encampments and knew of ancient trails used by the native people. These were some of the men introduced to Inginero Raul Ybarro (second from left), E. E. Townsend (second from right), and other members of the International Park Commission visiting San Carlos in 1936. (Photograph by George Grant, Courtesy of National Park Service.)

Two

THESE CAME AFTER

In 1885, the Estado Land and Cattle Company acquired Block G4 in Brewster County. The G4 Ranch extended from the Chisos Mountains to Terlingua Creek, and from the Rio Grande to Agua Fria and the Christmas Mountains. During the first years of operation, the ranch was stocked with 30,000 cattle, but by 1895, the ranch was disbanded due to drought and other problems. About 15,000 cattle were rounded up and shipped to market; the remaining wild herd was sold to smaller ranching operations. The large G4 was broken into smaller tracts, which was the beginning of a long trend of land subdivision.

Stories of cowboys and ranching abound in Big Bend and are still told around campfires by modern cowboys practicing eons-old, tried-and-true methods of managing herds. Tales of birth and death, bad weather and good times, and sweet girls and fancy things pass over the flames like winds over the landscape of time. But only a few have found ranching in the desert to be truly successful. Fickle nature with hailstorms, high winds, and sudden blue northers could take half the herd, leaving a family destitute. Drought and the Great Depression took many a rancher's dreams.

The story of the Fred Rice family illustrates one young couple's attempt at ranching in the Big Bend area. In an interview with Marc Rupert, in the *Alpine Avalanche*, Fred's son Frederick related his memories of ranch life in the Big Bend:

> Over the years, I have stood above the clouds on Emory Peak looking in awe upon the vast terrain of two countries sprawled out before me, and while sitting in a giant dagger's shade have felt the loneliness found on the wide expanse of Dagger Flat. I have made my way through early morning darkness to Lost Mine Peak and stared eastward awaiting the sun's first golden rays of light, and lost myself on purpose among the flaming slopes of Apache Canyon letting the world go on without me.

The land speaks with subtle wisdom for those who listen, and these words express the deeply spiritual impact Big Bend has on those who choose to open themselves to its voice.

In 1899, the Lucius Buttrill home was nestled into a canyon on the northwest side of the Rosillos Mountains, below one of the most abundantly flowing springs in Big Bend. Around the spring, they planted pecan and fruit trees. Hunting provided meat, and every household had a vegetable garden. Occasionally they slaughtered a cow or goat for meat. In the remote wilderness, there was no refrigeration, so meat was salted and dried or smoked to preserve it. The Buttrill home began with a simple adobe to which rooms were added, built of wood lumber that was shipped by wagon from Marathon. Today little remains to mark one of the earliest homesteads, save for a large pecan tree near the spring that stands as the emblem of this early ranching operation. (Courtesy of Nellie Rice.)

Lou and Anne Buttrill raised two daughters, Louanna and Marion. With no school in the vicinity, in 1910 they hired 26-year-old Effie Schley as governess to tutor the girls. Learning to ride, manage livestock around the ranch, and handle a firearm were all part of a young person's education. A large hat to protect against the sun was normal attire for anyone living in the desert. (Both courtesy of Nellie Rice.)

Fred Rice, one of Lou Buttrill's more romantic cowhands, began to like Effie Schley. Fred and Effie's locally famous horseback wedding took place in 1911 at the Buttrill's ranch. Neighbors and friends came from miles around for the event. Shown here are members of the Buttrill, Burnham, Nail, Seawell, Kibby, and Williams families, along with Rev. Charles Toddy. (Courtesy of Nellie Rice.)

The morning of the Rice wedding day on April 14, 1911, broke with overcast and somewhat foggy skies, and people bundled up for the outdoor wedding breakfast, served from the chuck wagon. (Courtesy of Nellie Rice.)

Rev. Charles Toddy from the Marathon Baptist Church presided over the wedding. The main participants in the ceremony rode horseback while Reverend Toddy read from scripture and Fred and Effie took their vows. (Courtesy of Nellie Rice.)

The wedding party made the Grand March, circling on horseback in celebration for the young couple. (Courtesy of Nellie Rice.)

After much ado, Fred and Effie left the wedding party behind and headed out on their honeymoon. (Courtesy of Nellie Rice.)

Young newlyweds, Fred and Effie stand at left with friends in Marathon next to their wagon of household possessions and ready to head south to their new ranch at Grapevine Hills. Fred and his brother, John Rice came to Big Bend in the early 1900s. They both worked for Lou Buttrill until they could make enough to purchase their own land. (Courtesy of Nellie Rice.)

Between 1910 and 1912, Worth Frazier helped Fred build the Grapevine Hills ranch house. The ranch was blessed with a rich flowing spring where cottonwoods, willows, and wild grapes flourished. John Rice settled near Chilicotal Spring, where several springs supplied sufficient water to maintain a ranching operation. Here they brought their families and strove to make a successful ranching operation. (Courtesy of Nellie Rice.)

In 1914, Fred and Effie were blessed with a son, Frederick, who grew up with the cool waters of Grapevine Spring that flowed into an orchard of fruit trees and a vegetable garden. Under the huge tree from which the family each year cut a branch for a Christmas tree, he learned lessons that would take him through the good and bad times of his later years. (Courtesy of Nellie Rice.)

Times were often difficult when weather would not cooperate. Disease struck the herds, panthers preyed on young livestock, or occasional rumors of bandits on the nearby border ran through homes. Despite trials, people made the best of bad times as well as the good. At left, Fred, holding his son Frederick, stands with two neighbors when a snowstorm provided the ice to use for homemade ice cream. By 1916, Fred and Effie had a daughter, Alice Bell (Allie B.) Rice, pictured below with Waddy Burnham's children at the Burnham Ranch. From left to right are Dorothy Burnham, Frederick, Allie B., Waddy Burnham Jr., and Evelyn Burnham. Tragically, in 1917, Effie died leaving Fred to manage two children and a ranch. At age 37, Fred married his second wife, Clara Mahaffey, who had been a teacher at Dugout Wells. (Both courtesy of Nellie Rice.)

The young Frederick Rice, at right, learned to ride from birth and thought nothing of a 20-mile journey to visit neighbors. San Vicente, 25 miles away, was simply a little farther ride than the next ranch. Anglo ranchers depended upon the local Mexican population for wranglers at roundup time. The Mexican adobe mason built the next addition to the house, and when sickness fell on a family member, the closest thing to a doctor was the local Mexican *curandero*, or healer. Below, Frederick in the center stands with compadres, William Starr at left and Liberato Gamboa on the right. Learning Spanish was as much a part of growing up as riding a horse or shooting a saddle rifle. (Both courtesy of Nellie Rice.)

The Great Depression hit hard for most ranchers who also had losses due to drought and severe weather. Fred Rice used Grapevine Ranch as collateral and moved to the old Dickey place near Dagger Flat. They built a large stone corral at Muskhog Spring. While Fred was working to keep a ranching business, his second wife, Clara, moved to Marathon with the children. Other more unfortunate ranchers were forced to leave the area entirely. (Courtesy of Nellie Rice.)

Three

SOME WERE HERE BEFORE

For Hispanics, their priorities include health, family, and friends and depending on circumstances, health often took third place. The "family" includes the extended family of grandparents, aunts, uncles, and cousins in need. Families instilled in their children the importance of honor, good manners, and respect for authority and the elderly. Preserving the Spanish language within the family remains a common mandate to preserve the cultural and family tradition today.

A firm handshake can be a congenial expression but can also be considered a signed contractual agreement. A hug and customary kiss on the cheek are also common greetings between women and men who are close friends or family.

Hispanics tend to be more relaxed and flexible about time and punctuality, and this tradition has been incorporated into the modern societal structure of Terlingua today in that not being on time is not only a socially acceptable behavior it is referred to locally as "Terlingua time."

In the Hispanic world, religion is a significant part of daily activity. The church influences family life and community affairs, giving spiritual meaning and cohesion to the culture. Where no church is available though and the priest only shows up once every six months, religious affairs are dealt with appropriately and reasonably. Catholicism in Terlingua tolerates other belief systems and actually incorporates them into ceremonial practice. Dia de los Muertos (Day of the Dead) is celebrated locally by Catholics, Protestants, and pagans, out of respect for those who have passed before, honoring their contribution to those things that confirm Terlingua's singular place in history.

The Rio Grande and its larger tributaries attracted farmers since prehistoric times. Mexicans established farms along the Rio Grande. These small operations were sufficient to supply the needs of their immediate group and productive enough to provide a surplus of food crops and livestock that could be traded for the other necessities. During the late 1800s, Mexican families reclaimed San Vicente, and by the 1890s, Boquillas, San Vicente, La Coyota, and Terlingua Abajo were well-established communities. The growth of Boquillas centered upon the discovery of lead, zinc, and silver ore in the Sierra del Carmen in Mexico. Opportunities for work in the mines spurred more settlement on both sides of the river. (Above photograph by Texas National Guard, below photograph by George Grant; both courtesy of the U.S. National Park Service.)

The mining industry had boom-or-bust periods as market prices fluctuated or when ore bodies were exhausted. The mines closed and people who remained in Boquillas turned to tourism for their main income. Other towns, like Terlingua, became ghost towns as people abandoned them in search of a better life elsewhere. In more recent times, this building in Boquillas, Mexico, was La Norteña Store. The Rio Grande has innumerable shallow places where park visitors have traditionally crossed into Boquillas and other villages to experience the relaxed atmosphere in the "land of Mañana." These informal crossings provided rare opportunities for Americans to easily experience the atmosphere of rural Mexico. (Photographs by George Grant; both courtesy of the U.S. National Park Service.)

At left, Don Juan and Doña Maria (Chata) Sada, well known Big Bend residents, maintained a modest business in Boquillas, Texas, providing food and beverages for anyone who visited the village. Chata's hospitality was renowned throughout the area and the couple was highly respected in Big Bend. Pictured below, Juan and Chata Sada stand in 1934 with some of their many foster children. (Both courtesy of the U.S. National Park Service.)

Jesús Estrada, the original owner of the farmland currently comprising Rio Grande Village, sold the land in 1918 to John O. Wedin, who raised sheep and irrigated the land to raise wheat. In 1926, Joe H. Graham purchased the farmland from Wedin to raise cattle and grow alfalfa for pasturage. Water pumped from the Rio Grande irrigated the farmland through a stone-lined acequia and distribution feeders across the area now comprising the Rio Grande Village. John Ringo Daniels purchased the farmland in the 1930s and worked the land until he lost it to the U.S. National Park Service in 1936. The park service modified these irrigation ditches to channel water to new campgrounds during the Mission 66 era. (Both courtesy of the U.S. National Park Service.)

Lupe Celaya, like many Mexicans, raised goats for milk and meat at San Vicente, Texas. To allow the adult goats to forage during the day, the young goats were kept in small shelters built of stone slabs where they could find shade from the sun. At night, the nannies came in to nurse the young goats. (Courtesy of Ross Maxwell Collection, U.S. National Park Service.)

At fiestas for religious ceremonies, social events, and family celebrations, a young goat was commonly slaughtered and cooked as the main course of the feast. Macario Hinojos (right) and his compadre are preparing this *cabrito* for just such a barbeque at Lajitas in 1945. (Courtesy of the U.S. National Park Service.)

The legendary Gilberto Luna, seen above, was of Mexican and American Indian blood and several sources list his age at death as 108. He outlived several wives and had numerous children and grandchildren. Luna lived and farmed along Alamo Creek by capturing seasonal flows from this normally dry creek to irrigate a modest farm. The family grew their own food, managed a small herd of goats, and Luna provided a freighting service, which supported the local economy. Luna delivered melons, vegetables, and cooked sotol to families at Chisos—the Hispanic reference to the Chisos Mine at Terlingua. Sotol is a traditional food plant that was gathered and consumed by American Indians, and its consumption among Hispanics locally is a testament to that culture's imprint within the Hispanic community. In the photograph below, Dr. Charles Gould, who studied plant ecology during the 1930s, captured this image of Pablo (left) and Ramon Celaya at their home in San Vicente, Texas. (Below photograph by Charles Gould; both courtesy of the U.S. National Park Service.)

The Great Depression took the nation by surprise and a decade passed before many people realized financial recovery. In Big Bend, marginal ranching operations that were heavily indebted to banks for loans on land, livestock, and livelihood found they could not overcome the diminishing buying power of the dollar, in spite of their hard work and commitment. Living on a frontier did not help because the distances to market increased the cost of living in a remote place. Many who chose desert life realized what it took to make it through the lean years, but drought in the mid-1930s compounded their financial troubles. The Molinar Ranch, located on Terlingua Creek in 1937, had adequate water and fared better than many. (Photograph by R.D. Roseberry, courtesy of the U.S. National Park Service.)

Around 1915, John Daniels and Mary (Maria) Daniels moved into the Chisos Mountains where they built a log cabin. They hauled everything up Blue Creek Canyon on a wagon and then up to Laguna Meadow on mules, including Haviland china, a dresser, and Maria's sewing machine. The Daniels depended heavily on deer hunting for meat but also maintained a bountiful garden. The Laguna was a large meadow that collected rainwater and provided lush grazing. When the Daniels' first daughter, May Sue, was born, they came down from the mountains for the birth but returned to their lives in the cool mountain heights. (Both courtesy of Ringo Smith.)

Tragedy struck when May Sue died at 14 months old. John and Maria moved to Boquillas, where they took up farming, but continued to use the mountain cabin. Maria was well known as high-spirited and intelligent, and after John's passing Maria continued as a storekeeper in Presidio. "Ma" Daniels, as she became known, was a resourceful trader throughout her life. (Courtesy of Ringo Smith.)

After a time, the Daniels were blessed with a second daughter, Jane Bandy Daniels. Pictured here dressed in traditional Mexican *quinceañera* (celebration of the 15th birthday) attire, Jane displays the spirit she inherited from her parents. (Courtesy of Ringo Smith.)

Some ranchers, like Waddy Burnham at Government Spring (above), were able to sustain themselves but with difficulty. Compounding the financial problems, some ranch women maintained households in Marathon for their children to attend school. John and his wife, Ida Avery Rice, had two sons (below), Albert, born in 1904, and Thomas, born a year later. John and Ida moved to a water hole near a canyon north of Dugout Wells that became known as Rice's Canyon. When they later moved to Chilicotal Spring, they left behind a cook stove that gave rise to the name Estufa (the Spanish word for stove) Canyon. Ida was a midwife for women in the area. (Above, courtesy of the U.S. National Park Service; below, Nellie Rice.)

Dugout Wells was a well-known stopover for people entering Big Bend during the early 20th century. Native Americans used this natural water source for millennia, and it lay along one route the Comanche Indians took into Mexico. The settlement here was never more than a half-dozen buildings, but wherever seven or more children lived, a public school could be established. Pictured above with their classmates at Dugout Wells School, sometime between 1915 and 1917, are Thomas Rice (lower center) and Albert Rice (lower right). The Dugout School was part of the broader San Vicente school district. The Dugout School house was a meeting hall for community events for residents living east of the Chisos Mountains. (Both courtesy of Nellie Rice.)

Many isolated ranches, lacking access to a school, relied on live-in teachers who worked for room and board and a nominal salary, teaching the few local children. Julia Nail was home-schooled on the ranch for three years by three different teachers. Miss Florence Pope, a recent master's degree graduate from Sul Ross State Teachers College, taught Julia and her neighbor Patricia Wilson. Above, from left to right are Miss Pope, Julia, Julia's mother Nina, and her father Sam Nail. To the right, Esta Fulcher was Julia's first live-in teacher. Some of the education involved rides around the ranch and observing nature in action. Julia's third teacher was Sarah Lee Todd, a cousin from Marathon. (Both courtesy of Julia Nail Moss.)

During hot summers, people shifted their work to the cooler parts of the day. Many homes had outdoor kitchens, and almost everyone slept outside during the summer. On especially hot summer days, a refreshing dip in the creek or, as in the image above, Sam Nail's water storage tank was a time for fun and relaxation. Pictured from left to right are Evelyn Burnham, Bill Burnham, Waddy T. Burnham, Dorothy Burnham, and Julia Nail. Below, many ranch children continued education at Sul Ross State College in Alpine, Texas. In the photograph are, from left to right, Julia Nail and classmates Rowena Armke, Charlotte Ward, and Bonnie Lou Pierce posing on the lawn of the Sul Ross campus. (Both courtesy of Julia Nail Moss.)

On the west side of the Chisos, Sam Nail and Homer Wilson operated sizeable ranches. Sam Nail's ranch, shown above, had a vegetable garden, a fruit-tree orchard, milk cows, and chickens. The well along Cottonwood Creek provided water. Today tall pecan trees and a windmill mark this ranch location along Ross Maxwell Scenic Drive in the park. The Chisos Mountains with deep canyons, tall shade trees, and abundant springs were a place where local ranchers could congregate and socialize, catch up on the latest happenings, and discuss future plans. At the picnic in the Chisos at right are, from left to right, Adele Haskell, Sarah Louise (Sally) Burnham, unidentified, Sam Nail, Waddy Burnham, Charlie Burnham, two unidentified people, Emmie Burnham, Sam's brother Jim Nail, and two unidentified friends. (Above, courtesy of Patricia Wilson Clothier; at right, Julia Nail Moss.)

At left, Francis Rooney originally purchased this mail-order house from Sears Roebuck and Company, had it shipped by rail to Marathon, and brought by wagon to the Nine Point Mesa Ranch. He later moved the house here to Oak Spring when he ranched on the west side of the Chisos Mountains. Homer Wilson acquired the ranch in 1929. The homesite benefited from spring water channeled to a small grove of fruit trees near the ranch house. The Wilsons lived here until 1944 when the park service acquired the land for inclusion in the park. Wilson raised Angora goats and maintained healthy rangeland by rotating herds and laying networks of water pipes carrying spring water to distant pastures. (At left, photograph by Glenn Burgess, courtesy of Archives of the Big Bend; below, Patricia Wilson Clothier.)

County-maintained roads made it easier to transport livestock and other products to and from the railway, benefiting ranches, mines, and other businesses. By the time Homer Wilson entered the ranching business, the well-maintained roads made it possible to contract shearing crews to come with their own equipment during shearing season. (At right, courtesy of Duncan Collection, Marfa and Presidio County Museum; below, photograph donated to the U.S. National Park Service by Dr. Walter Steiger, Big Bend National Park Archives.)

Waddy Burnham arrived in 1908. His ranch extended from the north side of the Chisos Mountains north to Paint Gap Hills, east to Grapevine Hills adjoining Fred Rice's ranch, and west to the Todd place at Croton Springs. According to Bill Burnham, one of Waddy Burnham Sr.'s kids, natural springs on the ranch had to be dug out occasionally to provide surface water for livestock. Waddy, like most ranchers in the area, ran Hereford cattle by preference, because the hardy breed endured the harsher desert conditions better than other breeds. (Above, courtesy of Julia Nail Moss; below, Duncan Collection, Marfa and Presidio County Museum.)

Pictured above at Sam Nail's ranch are members of the Emory Wilson family (no relation to Homer Wilson) in one of their first hunt camps around 1926. At right is Emory Wilson; sitting in the foreground with a pipe is Joe Wilson; standing, wearing goggles is Blanche Wilson; to the left of Blanche is her husband, Bryan; seated in front of them is Cecil Wilson; others in the photograph are unidentified members of their hunting party. Emory met Sam Nail at a cattle sale in Fort Worth and arranged to hunt on the Nail Ranch. Below, Blanche, young Tommy Wilson, and four unidentified men display their hunting success next to an ancient fallen cottonwood tree that once grew along Cottonwood Creek on Sam Nail's ranch. In the Depression years and since, ranchers found it necessary to supplement their operations by allowing hunters to use their ranches to generate income that the ranch alone could not provide. (Both courtesy of Bobby Wilson.)

Prior to the Mexican Revolution and the famous bandit raid on the Glenn Springs community, the candelilla wax factory, run by C. D. Woods, employed many Mexican workers. The community was divided, with the factory and Anglo residences on the east side of Glenn Draw and Mexican workers on the west. This dugout house was thatched with candelilla plants. (Photograph by Frank Duncan, courtesy of the Duncan Collection, Marfa and Presidio County Museum.)

More commonly, candelilla wax-rendering operations were small camps, temporarily set up near a water source. Most candelilla gatherers took care to not overharvest an area so it would be possible to return in a few years to resume wax processing. (Photograph by Glenn Burgess, courtesy of Clifford Casey Collection, Archives of the Big Bend.)

Four

THEY EXPERIENCED TURMOIL

Prior to the Mexican Revolution, many rural Mexicans lived under the hacendado system, essentially a serfdom where a wealthy landowner took advantage of the peones (serfs) and campesinos (peasant workers) to maintain large ranches or sometimes mining operations. The Constitution of 1917 abolished this system of servitude in favor of the *ejido* system, the communal use of land owned by the wealthy upper class. Many Mexicans fled to the United States to escape oppressive working conditions and turmoil of the revolution. The San Carlos crossing on the Rio Grande was a major path for Comanche warriors in the 19th century, and the Spanish military colony in San Carlos was a major stop along the trail for travelers going either south or north. Many Mexicans coming to work in mines in the United States passed through San Carlos.

The Mexican Revolution was a bloody and violent decade that created a general sense of ill ease along the border. By 1920, the government of Mexico achieved a degree of stability. Workers in the mining communities of Terlingua and Study Butte experienced very little threat from the *revolutionistas* across the border. After 1920, a number of families who fled the area returned to reestablish their livelihood.

829.
W.H. Horne Co.

1. Gen. Fierro.
2. Gen. Villa.
3. Gen. Ortega.
4. Col. Medina.

Increasing economic and social problems lead to the Mexican Revolution of 1910. In need of weapons and supplies, Mexican revolutionists made occasional raids across the U.S. border to plunder ranches and settlements in search of riding stock, weapons, and other supplies. According to E. E. Townsend, Francisco "Pancho" Villa had a stronghold in the Hechiceros Mountains, 30 miles south of Lajitas. The Mexican Revolution created a volatile and destabilizing decade, but by 1920, a more stable government arose in Mexico and the border conflict settled down. The years of violence made Anglos and Mexicans suspicious of one another, which intensified a distinct social and economic stratification along the border. (Above, photograph by W. H. Horne, National Archives and Records Administration, Record Group 165; below, photograph by C. Tucker Beckett, National Archives and Records Administration, Record Group 165.)

Mexican Rurales.

Small detachments of cavalry and infantry spaced along the border represented only a token military presence. Ten soldiers from Troop A of the 14th Cavalry were on patrol at Glenn Springs when on May 5, 1916, Mexican bandits raided the small community, resulting in the deaths of three soldiers and the son of the local storekeeper. Following this and other raids, the U.S. War Department enlarged the camp and created other outposts to protect border settlements. (Above, courtesy of the Museum of the Big Bend; below, the U.S. National Park Service.)

In 1919, the United States contracted with Howard Perry and Wayne Cartledge to lease land at Castolon in order to establish a permanent outpost. To replace their temporary quarters, the construction division contracted for the building of permanent barracks and other structures. During this construction, the war in Europe and the conflict along the border subsided and much of the planned work at Castolon was suspended. By 1920, most troops were reassigned, and the camp was soon abandoned. (Photograph by Texas National Guard, courtesy of the U.S. National Park Service.)

Five

THEY CAME SEEKING WEALTH

After the Big Bend became part of the United States in 1848, adventurous explorers trickled into this remote frontier searching for instant wealth. By the late 1800s, prospectors had discovered rich lead, zinc, and silver deposits in the Sierra del Carmen of Coahuila, Mexico, and silver in Shafter, north of Presidio. In the small village of Boquillas, Coahuila, a smelter processed ore for delivery across the river to markets in the United States. In 1894, Edward Lindsey set up operations to receive ore from the Mexican side and Boquillas, Texas, developed on the Texas side of the river.

Cinnabar is a rich crimson-colored mineral from which mercury, or quicksilver, is extracted by heating ore in a furnace and condensing the liquid metal from hot vapor. Various mining companies built numerous retorts during the 50-year history of mercury mining in the Terlingua Mining District. The Chisos Mining Company, established in 1903 by Howard Perry, was the most successful in the district and was responsible for 60 percent of the 150,000 flasks produced in the area. The two world wars spurred high demand for mercury, which was used in the production of explosives.

Corruption, claim jumping, and financial disaster, typical of mining ventures worldwide, were certainly true in the Big Bend. One example was the discovery in the 1890s of cinnabar by Martín Solis, a successful rancher and storekeeper who lived east of Mariscal Mountain. According to the family's history, Solis presented a sample of ore to Ed Lindsey for analysis. Lindsey—realizing the potential for wealth—promptly filed on the discovery himself. Through errors in land surveying, Lindsey lost his claim to the Sanger Brothers of Dallas, Texas, who operated the mine until 1908 when a sudden drop in the price of quicksilver forced them to focus operations at the Dallas Mine in Study Butte. Eventually W. K. Ellis acquired the workings and constructed the first processing plant, which operated until 1919. Like many mining ventures, a string of ownerships typified the history of Mariscal and the other mining enterprises in Terlingua.

During the 1890s, prospectors discovered deposits of lead, zinc, and silver in the Sierra del Carmen in Coahuila, Mexico. Under direction of the Kansas City Smelting and Refining Company (KSARCO), the Puerto Rico and Zaragoza Mines for a period produced rich ore that was transported across the Rio Grande. High-grade zinc and lead-silver ore accumulated at the mine entrance where it awaited transport to the ore tramway. (Both courtesy of the U.S. National Park Service.)

Towers made from 16-inch-thick timbers supported a cable system that carried ore from a loading terminal high on the Sierra del Carmen across the Rio Grande to an off-loading terminal 6 miles away. From the discharge terminal in Texas, wagons delivered ore to the railway in Marathon to be shipped to the KSARCO smelter in El Paso, Texas. (Both courtesy of the U.S. National Park Service.)

After Lindsey lost his quicksilver operation at Mariscal, W. K. Ellis began extracting and processing the rich deposits in 1916. The Ellis processor was a simple retort to heat the cinnabar ore and clay pipe tubes to condense the mercury vapors for collection into cast-iron flasks. (Courtesy of Ross Maxwell Collection, U.S. National Park Service.)

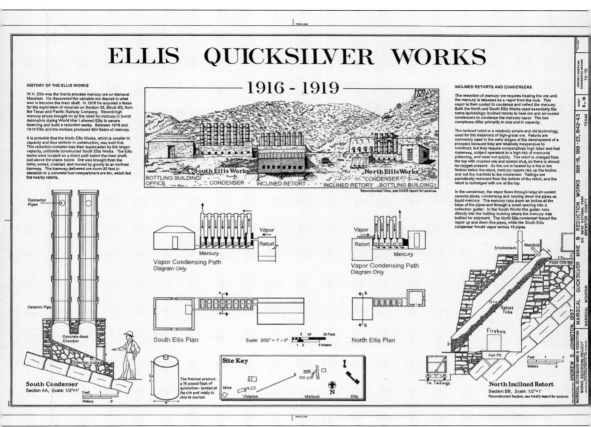

Between 1917 and 1919, the Ellis Mine produced 894 flasks of quicksilver, but Ellis failed to keep up his interest payments. By 1919, the land reverted to the state of Texas. The rapid increases in the price of quicksilver during World War I brought a rush of prospectors into Big Bend. (Courtesy of the Historic American Engineering Record, U.S. National Park Service.)

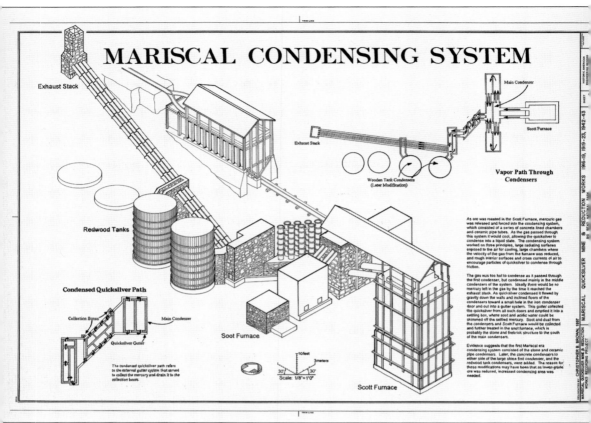

Under the management of W. D. Burcham, Mariscal Mine operated from 1919 to 1923, employing between 20 and 40 men. Most were Mexican nationals who came from San Luis Potosi and the Sierra Mojada mining districts in Mexico. More experienced workers earned $1.50 per 10-hour day. Lesser-skilled workers made $1 to $1.25 per 10-hour day, 6 days per week. Their pay usually returned to the company through the company commissary. The elaborate but inefficient processing plant was slow to produce, and the expense of building and operating it outweighed production profits. Eventually the properties of the Mariscal Mining Company were sold at public auction to cover litigation against the company. (Courtesy of the Historic American Engineering Record, U.S. National Park Service.)

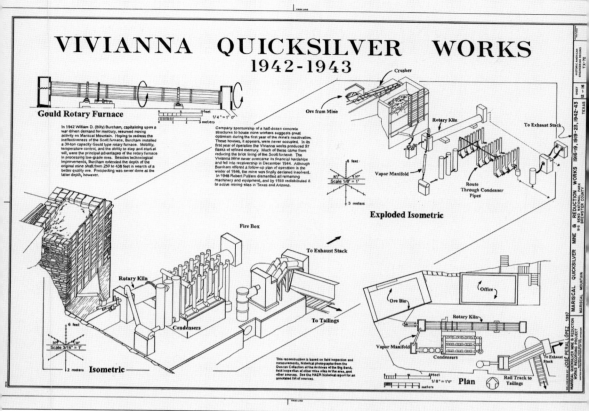

VIVIANNA QUICKSILVER WORKS
1942-1943

Gould Rotary Furnace

Crusher

Ore from Mine

Rotary Kiln

To Exhaust Stack

Vapor Manifold

Route Through Condenser Pipes

Exploded Isometric

Fire Box

To Exhaust Stack

Rotary Kiln

Condensers

To Tailings

Office

Ore Bin

Rotary Kiln

Vapor Manifold

Condensers

To Exhaust Stack

Rail Track to Tailings

Isometric

Plan

During World War I and World War II, the quicksilver industry thrived. In 1942, W. D. Burcham organized the Vivianna Mining Company, secured the lease, and reopened the old Mariscal Mine. During World War II, the Vivianna Mine, with a new 30-ton-capacity Gould furnace, began production at Mariscal Mountain. Many workers brought their families and at first built temporary dugout houses and simple jacals until more permanent rock houses were constructed. After the closing of Mariscal Mine, most workers moved to the Study Butte and Terlingua Mines. (Courtesy of the Historic American Engineering Record, U.S. National Park Service.)

Between 1942 and 1943, the price of quicksilver declined. New owners salvaged this equipment and moved the Gould furnace to the Maggi Mine in the Terlingua Mining District. (Courtesy of W. J. Burcham Collection, Archives of the Big Bend.)

Between World War I and World War II, W. D. Burcham managed operations at the Study Butte Mine, which had, pictured from left to right, a Scott furnace, a large primary condenser, and six secondary condensers. The furnace needed 1.5 cords of wood per day. During a 31-month period, the mine bought over 2,500 cords of wood, costing between $4.50 and $10 per cord. About one-fourth of the wood was hauled from Castolon, La Coyota, and Terlingua Abajo. (Data provided by Bob Wirt, photograph courtesy of W. J. Burcham Collection, Museum of the Big Bend.)

Most workers in the mines in Terlingua and Study Butte came from areas of northern Mexico and found favorable conditions and productive livelihoods in the United States. At Terlingua, families had access to a doctor, a school, and the best store in the area. Many elderly speak fondly of those days when they considered themselves fortunate to have such a good life. (Above courtesy of W. J. Burcham Collection, Museum of the Big Bend; below María Zamarron Bermudez; additional contributions, Cynta de Narvaez.)

Martín Zamarron and others clean up after a fire at a Chisos Mine building. The Hispanic people, with ethics of hard work and dedication, provided the power to sustain commercial endeavors throughout the Big Bend area. Their service was often given in the background and their intense labor often went unrecognized, except for their families who realized the personal rewards of hard work. (Courtesy of María Zamarron Bermudez.)

Hispanics working Perry's Chisos Mine called this community Chisos. There were weekly dances, a Catholic church, a movie theater (the building with a white facade), and an ice cream shop. Occasionally a "supplier" came through selling sotol and tequila. (Courtesy of María Zamarron Bermudez; additional contributions, Cynta de Narvaez.)

These people who had known nothing but hardship in Old Mexico found a safe place where they could enjoy their lives and prosper. To María Zamarron Bermudez, Terlingua was a very nice place to live. María, about 14 years old at the time of the above photograph, is seated at left with her cousin Beatrice Chacon (center) and Julia Vasquez Chavez on the porch of the Chisos Hotel where Maria worked as housekeeper. In recent years, a locally organized reunion called Viva la Historia brought many of the families of the Chisos miners back to Terlingua to once again revive and tell their family histories. (Both courtesy of María Zamarron Bermudez; additional contributions, Cynta de Narvaez.)

Terlingua Abajo and La Coyota supplied garden crops for workers of Terlingua and wood for the mine furnaces. While men toiled in fields and mines, women bore children, healed the sick, and fed the hungry. Seen at right (from left to right), Juliana Chavarria, Maria Galindo Chavarria, Antolina Chavarria Rojo, and Santos Franco (child) lived at La Coyota, a little-known community along the river that helped sustain Terlingua. Below, at the Chavarria home around 1919, from left to right are (sitting) Feliz Valenzuela (who became constable), Chamano Catáno, and Paz Molinar; (standing) Antonio Franco, Patricio Marquez, Bernardo Garcia, and Sixto Chavarria. No one deserved time to celebrate more than the people who, through their labor, held together the Big Bend. To raise a glass with these men would be an honor. (Both Chavarria family photographs, courtesy of Mr. Alejandro and Mrs. Estefana Sandate and Museum of the Big Bend.)

Surnames like Franco, Garcia, Chavarria, Martinez, Valenzuela, and Molinar are well known in Big Bend, and as a person walks through the cemeteries of Big Bend, history lies at his or her feet. The Dia de los Muertos, or Day of the Dead, is an annual celebration of the lives of those who have passed on before, when the community turns out to clean and decorate the cemetery and take part in a feast commemorating the lives of the ancestors. (Photograph by author.)

Six

THEY WANTED
TO CONSERVE

After World War I and the failure of the Hoover administration in curbing the economic devastation of the Great Depression, Franklin D. Roosevelt's economic recovery plan, the New Deal, instituted unprecedented large-scale federal relief programs aimed at aiding the struggling agricultural and manufacturing industries. In 1933, the Civilian Conservation Corps (CCC) was established and put hundreds of young Americans to work on conservation programs on federal, state, and municipal lands across the nation.

The U.S. National Park Service found itself filling a need of the American public for places of recreation. After the establishment of an international peace park joining the United States and Canada, a desire arose to establish a similar park connecting the United States and Mexico.

As early as 1921, a group of individuals petitioned the state legislature to consider establishing a state park in the Davis Mountains. Several visionary citizens stimulated interest in a park in the Chisos Mountains during this time, and in 1935 they proposed the establishment of Big Bend National Park. Legislation authorizing and establishing the park was finally passed in 1944. Although the international peace park idea has occasionally resurfaced during the past 70 years, it has yet to reach fruition.

Everett Townsend is generally credited as the father of Big Bend National Park, but the idea was shared earlier in 1924, when Alpine doctor and state senator Benjamin F. Berkeley proposed establishing a park in the Chisos Mountains. Here Senator Berkeley (far left) is seated with his family at his cottage near present day Rio Grande Village. (Photograph donated to the U.S. National Park Service by Dr. Walter Steiger, courtesy of the U.S. National Park Service.)

Posing here in 1933 from left to right, U. S. Congressman Robert Ewing Thomason, president of Alpine Chamber of Commerce John W. Gillette, secretary of the Brewster County Chamber of Commerce A. F. Robinson, and rancher Sam R. Nail met to discuss the potential park in the Chisos Mountains. Congressman Thomason sponsored a bill that on June 20, 1935, became Public Law No. 157 establishing Big Bend National Park. (Courtesy of National Park Service.)

In 1937, Texas governor James V. Allred directed the Texas National Guard to photograph Big Bend. In a letter dated December 26, 1937, transmitting a set of aerial photographs to Everett Townsend, Allred wrote, "Since you are the real 'Daddie' of the Big Bend idea, I think it only fitting you should have these pictures." These spectacular images, provided to the U.S. National Park Service, influenced the early planning for the park. (Letter from E. E. Townsend collection, courtesy of Archives of the Big Bend; image courtesy of the U.S. National Park Service.)

In January 1934, Roger Toll spent three days inspecting the area with historian J. Evetts Haley, E. E. Townsend, John W. Gillette, rancher Homer Wilson, and others. Toll remarked that one needed a month to study all parts of the area and commented on the remarkably spectacular view from the South Rim. At this outstanding feature, the cliffs plunge abruptly, dropping 2,600 feet in a horizontal mile. (Courtesy of National Park Service.)

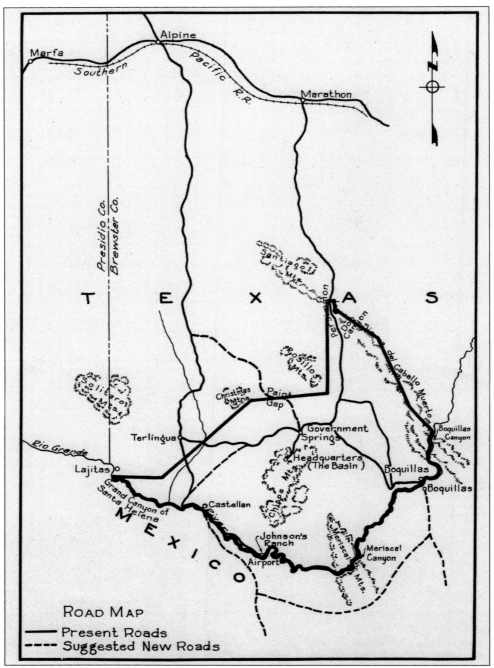

The Boundary Line Report, Big Bend National Park Project, by Conrad Wirth, dated September 9, 1935, described the findings of an expedition by various specialists into the Chisos and surrounding area. The Chisos was determined to be a uniquely complete biological unit—an ecological island worthy of protection. The park contained unparalleled geological phenomena and scenic qualities suitable for inclusion in the U.S. National Park system. (Courtesy of the U.S. National Park Service.)

Following a series of international conferences between the U.S. and Mexico on the concept of an international park, representatives from federal, state, and local interests converged at Alpine, Texas, and a landmark expedition entered the park, touring both sides of the international border February 15–23, 1936. On February 19, the group gathered at the home of Juan and Chata Sada in Boquillas, Texas, preparing to cross into the proposed Mexican protected area. (Both photographs by George Grant, courtesy of the U.S. National Park Service.)

After a grueling drive across the Rio Grande into the Fronteriza range (the southern extent of the Sierra del Carmen), the group arrived at Rancho San Isidro, the home of Jaime Vela Garcia, in Canyon de los Alamos, Coahuila, Mexico. (Both photographs by George Grant, courtesy of the U.S. National Park Service.)

On February 20, the group rode horseback to the top of the heavily forested Fronteriza range and looked over a spectacular view from Vaca Peak. The idea of the Fronteriza and the Chisos as ecological islands was intensely discussed during this time. On February 21, the group returned to their camp in the Chisos and on February 22 crossed the Rio Grande at Lajitas en route to another part of proposed Mexican protected area southwest of Sierra Santa Helena. (Both photographs by George Grant, courtesy of the U.S. National Park Service.)

Tragedy struck within 24 hours of the dispersal of the International Park Commission when Roger Toll and George Wright died in an automobile accident. Losing the leadership skills of these men set development of the international park idea back, and losing their inspiration for scientific inquiry marked the beginning of a decline in the U.S. National Park Services science program. In 1933, Robert M. Wagstaff and Everett Townsend coauthored state House Bill No. 771 to create Texas Canyons State Park. On May 27 of that year, the bill was passed with minor changes; principally the name would be changed to Big Bend State Park. On May 21, 1934, the first 200-member CCC crew arrived in the Chisos Basin. (Below, from the John Wurz Collection; both courtesy of the U.S. National Park Service.)

The first orders were to improve the road into the Chisos Mountains and construct buildings to replace the tent camp. Seven miles of primitive two-track road were engineered and completely reconstructed by hand labor, including building over 30 concrete and stone culverts and bridges spanning the numerous washes that the road must cross to reach the Chisos Basin. The equipment available to the CCC frequently broke down as they attempted to cross Panther Pass into the basin, and a mechanical workshop was set up on the Green Gulch side of the pass. (Both courtesy of John Wurz Collection, National Park Service.)

Hispanics and African Americans made up over 80 percent of the first CCC work crew in Big Bend. These dedicated men worked elbow to elbow moving tons of earth and rock to create the road that is now used to reach the Chisos Basin. The CCC also built trails to Lost Mine and the Window and started work on two other trails. Each of these trails has extensive stonework that typifies the rustic architectural style common to the CCC. (Above, from the John Wurz Collection; below, image purchased from Peter Koch by the U.S. National Park Service; both courtesy of the U.S. National Park Service.)

By 1936, superintendent R. D. Morgan, seated in the center in the image above, had a crew of foremen and scientific specialists who conducted the first major research on the resources of Big Bend National Park. Standing, fourth from the left, is junior geologist Ross A. Maxwell, who later became the first superintendent of the park as well as a major contributing author to the seminal geological study, published in 1967 by the Bureau of Economic Geology at the University of Texas. Pictured below from left to right are regional biologist William B. McDougall, biologist Ardry Borell, Ross Maxwell, Waddy Burnham, Juan Gamboa (guide), and Charles Gould after their pack trip into the Dead Horse Mountains investigating the rich biological and geologic resources. McDougall, Gould, and Maxwell were among the first scientists to chart in detail this last frontier. (Both courtesy of Ross Maxwell Collection, U.S. National Park Service.)

The CCC camp house museum displays the extensive collections from these early scientific expeditions. Tragedy struck in 1941 when an oil-heater fire burned the CCC museum entirely to the ground with an immeasurable loss of the priceless specimens people had worked so hard to accumulate. (Both courtesy of Ross Maxwell Collection, National Park Service.)

Seven

VESTIGES

Big Bend National Park was established for its scenic qualities and recreational opportunities. During the first decade of the park, management wrestled with the problems of managing a huge piece of landscape with far too few employees. One superintendent, one ranger, and a couple of maintenance staff struggled to make the park a pleasant place for visitors coming from across the nation. Park operations were set up in the abandoned CCC camp. Employees renovated these rustic buildings to make them more habitable by families with children. A simple campground was carved out of the area disturbed by the construction of the CCC camp.

National Park Concessions, Inc. was contracted to build and operate lodging and restaurant facilities in the Chisos Basin. Dallas Huts salvaged from Oak Ridge, Tennessee, were the original lodging for park guests. These buildings served as living and workspace for both concessions operations and National Park Service (NPS) staff until the late 1970s.

In the mid-1950s, the NPS began a nationwide park infrastructure modernization program, with a completion deadline of 1966. The Mission 66 program, as it was called, began its early years in Big Bend National Park and historians consider the Mission 66 development in Big Bend to be prototypical of Mission 66 design. Mission 66 facilities serve the park today.

During the first decades of the park, the NPS dismantled many abandoned structures under a policy of returning the park to a natural state. Some buildings suffered from serious structural failure and their destruction removed safety hazards. After the passing of the National Historic Preservation Act of 1966, the NPS developed a program to preserve buildings and sites considered to have historic or architectural significance. This chapter begins by depicting many structures that no longer exist and brings the reader to the modern parkscape.

The CCC camp in the Chisos Basin was abandoned at the beginning of World War II. The NPS set up operations here in the mid-1940s and operated park headquarters from the basin until construction began at Panther Junction during the Mission 66 era (1955–1966). The building seen below served as the main ranger station during the first years of park operations. In the early days, the park was administered with less than a handful of people. (Above, photograph by Texas National Guard, U.S. National Park Service; both courtesy of the U.S. National Park Service.)

Park Ranger and Mrs. Orin P. Senter are working on their living quarters to make them more habitable. Simple acts of adding curtains to the windows, a fence to keep javelinas out of the flower beds, and some lawn chairs on the porch made living in these basic quarters tolerable. (Both courtesy of the U.S. National Park Service.)

At the close of World War II, superintendent Maxwell obtained about $84,000 worth of War Assets Administration surplus. The park acquired road construction and maintenance equipment, trucks, pickups, power plants, powered shop tools, numerous varieties of hand tools, and considerable quantities of building materials and supplies. Rancher Lloyd Wade worked with the Civilian Conservation Corps during early park development and was caretaker of the CCC camp after it was abandoned in 1941. Wade continued to work as maintenance foreman during the early years of the park. Seen below in 1945, he is repairing the park's automotive equipment. (Both courtesy of the U.S. National Park Service.)

Dallas Huts, prefabricated structures assembled in the field as a kit, were commonly used during World War II. In 1946, superintendent Maxwell brought 21 of these Dallas Huts to the Chisos Basin, where National Park Concessions, Inc. (NPCI) began meal service, and opened a store and service station. Their operation took over four CCC housekeeping cottages and a second small building, using them as a grocery store, restaurant, and kitchen. The Chuck Wagon was a cool getaway on a hot summer day, providing meals, cold beverages, and a meeting place where visitors could swap stories. (Both photographs by W. Ray Scott, courtesy of National Park Concessions, Inc.)

Eventually the Dallas Hut cabins, seen above, were replaced by the modern motel building shown under construction in the image below. Photographer W. Ray Scott skillfully captured the Dallas Huts in the background being replaced by modern architecture. (Above, courtesy of the U.S. National Park Service; below, photograph by W. Ray Scott, courtesy of National Park Concessions, Inc.)

NPCI operated this gasoline station in the basin until the NPS removed it in the 1980s. By 1959, modern electric gas pumps replaced the original glass reservoir type. (Above, photograph by W. Ray Scott, courtesy of National Park Concessions, Inc.; below, photograph by Jack Boucher, courtesy of the U.S. National Park Service.)

The Chisos Basin Store, built in 1940 by the CCC, served as the campers' store and reservation office for the Dallas Hut cabins until the construction of the main lodge building in the 1960s. It continued to serve as the campers' store until the NPS removed it in the 1980s. (Photograph by W. Ray Scott, courtesy of National Park Concessions, Inc.)

Bill Cooper operated stores in five locations near Persimmon Gap. This is the appearance of the Cooper Store near Dog Canyon in 1956 before the NPS removed the abandoned building. (Photograph by Harold J. Brodrick, courtesy of the U.S. National Park Service.)

Like many buildings abandoned when the NPS took over in the 1940s, the roof of Johnson's Trading Post began deteriorating and was in imminent danger of collapse. The trading post was not completely dismantled, but the roof framing was removed to eliminate a safety hazard and the adobe walls were allowed to slowly melt into the desert. The Works Progress Administration operated for a short time from the building, seen below, at Johnson's Ranch. This structure was demolished in 1953. (Both courtesy of the U.S. National Park Service.)

Chata and Juan Sada operated a restaurant and store from the above home during the early decades of the 20th century. During the 1930s, numerous international dignitaries, scientists, and celebrities promoting the international peace park congregated at Chata's place prior to traveling into Mexico. Below, in 1939, this group of park service planners and architects visited the park to discuss CCC development in the Chisos. From left to right are regional architect Harvey Cornell, associate regional architect Lyle Bennett, Carlos Mendoza, Ralph Lassiter, Chata Sada, regional director M.R. Tillotson, O. G. Taylor, and planning inspector Tom Boles. (Both courtesy of the U.S. National Park Service.)

An entire volume could be written about the influence the Sadas had on the area. In August 1956, Mexicans from Boquillas, Mexico, were allowed to dismantle and salvage material from Chata's place. In December of that year, the U.S. National Park Service employees leveled the remains of Chata's place. (Both courtesy of the U.S. National Park Service.)

The Burnham family, who headquartered their ranch at Government Spring, built this home after their first house burned. Park service employees used this building for social functions until a shortage of operating funds could no longer support its upkeep. The building was destroyed in the 1970s due to lack of funds to maintain it. (Courtesy of the U.S. National Park Service.)

Historic buildings such as Robert Serna's K-Bar Ranch House (seen here), Barker Lodge at Rio Grande Village, and the Castolon Officers Quarters were dedicated to house visiting researchers. Due to recent funding shortages, the NPS found it necessary to convert all but K-Bar for use as employee housing. (Photograph by Robert M. Utley, courtesy of the U.S. National Park Service.)

For millennia, American Indians considered the healing waters of the Hot Springs sacred. They set aside their differences so that everyone could share this natural wonder. John O. Langford arrived at the Hot Springs in 1909 and set up a resort operation centered around the healing qualities of the springs. This building served as a store, post office, and general meeting place in the Boquillas community. Langford, with the help of local Mexican labor, built a row of cabins where visitors could relax during their stay at Hot Springs. The Hot Springs site is on the National Register of Historic Places. (Above, photograph by Natt Dodge; both courtesy of the U.S. National Park Service.)

Maggie Smith, who operated the store at Hot Springs, moved from the Hot Springs to San Vicente, Texas, and operated this store until the late 1950s when the property was finally acquired by the U.S. National Park Service. (Photograph by Harold J. Brodrick, courtesy of the U.S. National Park Service.)

Pictured here in the early 1950s, storekeeper Maggie Smith and an unidentified man discuss the differences in the Mexican style of saddle. (Photograph by Glenn Burgess, Courtesy Clifford Casey Papers, Archives of the Big Bend.)

Boquillas, Texas, across the Rio Grande from Boquillas, Coahuila, once formed the core of a more widespread community loosely referred to as Boquillas. This community occupied both sides of the river and supported several hundred residents. A school in the upper right, Chata and Juan Sada's store at middle right, and a scattering of other buildings once stood at this town site. The Barker Lodge buildings, at center, are the only remaining structures from the village of Boquillas, Texas. (Photograph by W. Ray Scott, courtesy of National Park Concessions, Inc.)

Wayne Cartledge operated La Harmonia Company, centered on cotton production at Castolon. Around 1900, Cipriano Hernandez, a successful Hispanic entrepreneur from Camargo, Chihuahua, built the Alvino House (lower right). Hernandez farmed, ranched, and operated several stores between Castolon and Terlingua Abajo until the 1940s. The Alvino House stands today as a testimony to the industrious Hispanic culture of the Big Bend. (Courtesy of the U.S. National Park Service.)

After Camp Santa Helena was abandoned by the U.S. Army in 1920, Wayne Cartledge purchased the buildings and operated the La Harmonia Company here until the U.S. National Park Service acquired the property in 1961, when this photograph was taken. National Parks Concessions, Inc. continued the operation of the store until 2001 when the contract was reassigned to Forever Resorts. (Photograph by Harold J. Brodrick, courtesy of the U.S. National Park Service.)

Between Castolon and Santa Elena Canyon, the Sublett Farm National Register Historic District preserves remnants of the Grand Canyon Company, a farming operation established in 1918 as a partnership between James Sublett and Albert Dorgan. When this image was taken in 1945, these irrigated fields in the Rio Grande floodplain produced garden crops for Castolon and Terlingua. (Photograph by Natt Dodge, courtesy of the U.S. National Park Service.)

James L. Sublett built his adobe home on the elevated mesa where it could capture cooling breezes. Typical of homes in this era, Sublett used naturally available materials to build shade ramadas for protection against the sun's heat. Grand Canyon farms, for a brief time, pulled water from the Rio Grande via a waterwheel that transferred irrigation water to a main canal that carried the precious liquid over 1.5 miles to the fields. The waterwheel was replaced by a gasoline-powered centrifugal pump. (Courtesy of James Sublett Collection, U.S. National Park Service.)

This image of the Sublett's adobe, taken in 1952, shows that the house had grown in size to meet the needs of the family. The simple ramadas from the 1920s had been replaced with store-bought lumber. The foundation is all that remains of the Sublett adobe farmhouse. (Courtesy of the U.S. National Park Service.)

This house, designed by Albert Dorgan and built by Mexican labor, contained several unique architectural features including large cottonwood lintels above recessed windows. Several rooms surrounded a large parlor that opened onto a patio with a spectacular view overlooking the river. In the center of the parlor was a massive fireplace made of local petrified wood. Large cottonwood tree trunks spanned between the fireplace and the four adjacent corners and supported the roof. In the 1950s, the roof was removed and the building began to deteriorate. In the 1990s, the NPS Vanishing Treasures program funded the preservation of the front architectural elements visible in this 1951 photograph. (Courtesy of the U.S. National Park Service.)

The most singular vernacular structure in the park is Luna's Jacal. Gilberto Luna built this humble home at his farm on Alamo Creek where he captured seasonal runoff from the creek and channeled it to his fields. The only visible evidence that anyone lived in this seemingly desolate location is his rustic house, built in unique fashion to extend out from a huge boulder. By 1959, Luna's Jacal was suffering from years of neglect, and in the late 1960s, the NPS reconstructed it to match its original appearance. Luna's Jacal is on the National Register of Historic Places. (Below, photograph by Jack Boucher; both courtesy of the U.S. National Park Service.)

At Mariscal Mining District, the Vivianna Mining operation had difficulty extracting ore quickly enough to keep the Gould furnace operating efficiently and workers dismantled the old Mariscal Mine's Scott furnace (at lower left), feeding the mercury-laden bricks into the Gould furnace. Today the ruins of the old Mariscal Mine dominate the scene. (Courtesy of the Historic American Engineering Record, U.S. National Park Service.)

The Persimmon Gap Entrance Station, pictured here as it appeared in 1953, was one of five locations where Bill Cooper operated a store. This building is the first man-made structure to greet visitors who enter the park from Marathon. (Photograph by George Grant, courtesy of U.S. National Park Service.)

This rock and adobe building was built in the early 1940s by the Civilian Conservation Corps. For about 30 years, National Parks Concessions, Inc. operated their reservation office and camper store here. In the 1950s, Dallas Huts were added to the back to provide shower and bathroom facilities for park visitors. The store also served as the Chisos Basin Post Office. These buildings were removed by the NPS during the 1990s. (Courtesy of the U.S National Park Service.)

In the Chisos Basin, the Chisos Mountains Lodge dining room, built during the Mission 66 era of the 1960s, serves visitors today with a varied menu. The view west toward the Window and the distance beyond provides many visitors the opportunity to enjoy spectacular sunsets while they dine. (Photograph by W. Ray Scott, courtesy of National Park Concessions, Inc.)

Stone Cottage 102 is one of four completed around 1940 by the CCC. These are the most popular lodge units in the basin, usually reserved over a year in advance. The units originally had kerosene heaters until electricity came to the basin in the late 1950s. (Both photographs by W. Ray Scott, courtesy of National Park Concessions, Inc.)

The Homer Wilson Ranch Blue Creek headquarters was determined eligible for listing in the National Register of Historic Places. This historic site provides an opportunity for today's visitors to view these rustic vernacular structures by stopping for a short hike as they travel the Ross Maxwell Scenic Drive. (Courtesy of the U.S. National Park Service.)

Along the Ross Maxwell Scenic Drive, the Sam Nail historic site provides a short hike into a tranquil and bucolic setting beneath a working windmill, nestled among tall pecan trees and native Mexican walnuts. The Nail's ranch house has, over the years, slowly melted into the desert as vegetation reclaims its dominance. A windmill, periodically maintained by the park service, continues to mechanically chant a song of long-ago pioneers who settled the land, lived with the land, and were disappointed to leave their love of this enchanting desert behind. (Photograph by Robert M. Utley, courtesy of the U.S. National Park Service.)

The major infusion of funds during the Mission 66 era provided the park with many modern facilities that continue to serve today. Housing was constructed at Panther Junction, Rio Grande Village, and the Chisos Basin. During Mission 66, the park service planted ash, cottonwood, and sycamore trees throughout Rio Grande Village. (Photograph by Harold J. Brodrick, courtesy of the U.S. National Park Service.)

Park employees and their families are pictured celebrating Arbor Day. In this image, Mr. and Mrs. McCune Ott and their twin daughters, Kristy and Kathy finish planting the 10,000th tree at Rio Grande Village. (Photograph by Harold J. Brodrick, courtesy of the U.S. National Park Service.)

The original irrigation system that evolved during the 1920s and 1930s was enhanced during the 1950s under Mission 66 to feed water to new campgrounds and picnic areas. These obscure structures are occasionally discovered by park visitors but most are completely unaware of their contribution to the history of the development of Big Bend National Park. (Both photographs by Harold J. Brodrick, courtesy of the U.S. National Park Service.)

The Mission 66 improvements included massive road reconstruction, paving, and construction of two large bridges spanning Tornillo Creek. In 1959, a through-mountain tunnel was built at Rio Grande Village. This tunnel still frames a spectacular view of the Sierra del Carmen in Mexico for motorists entering the Rio Grande Village developed area. (Above, photograph by Jack Boucher; below, photograph by Harold J. Brodrick; both courtesy of the U.S. National Park Service.)

In the Chisos Basin campground, the park service built ramadas to cover tables and charcoal broilers. Sanitary facilities and sites for tents and trailers were available for years without cost. Due to budget constraints, the U.S. National Park Service had to start charging fees for camping. More recently, it became necessary to charge an entrance fee for the park. (Photograph by Jack Boucher, courtesy of the U.S. National Park Service.)

The campfire circle or amphitheater is a favorite with the visitors to Big Bend National Park. In the evening, a small but cheerful blaze provided the background for the naturalist talks and slide-film presentations. This circle, completed under the NPS Mission 66 program, provides seating for 250 persons. Unfortunately the campfire is no longer continued as a part of evening interpretive programs that are conducted here by the park service. (Photograph by Jack Boucher, Courtesy of National Park Service.)

The San Vicente School, with its long history in south Brewster County, found a permanent home at Panther Junction and a new set of classrooms. The nearest school was in Marathon or Alpine, an extreme distance of 70 to 100 miles. Many ranchers considered it routine to maintain households in these towns to provide education for their children. The park employees contended with this problem until recent years when a kindergarten-through-high school was established in Terlingua. Quality education in this remote area remains a concern for park employees, concession employees, and other local residents. (Courtesy of the U.S. National Park Service.)

The first day of school in the new building was an enjoyable event for teachers and students alike. The prospect of not having to make the long drive to Marathon, or for a spouse to not have to maintain a separate household in Marathon during the school year, was a welcomed blessing. (Courtesy of the U.S. National Park Service.)

Above, the dedication of the Mission 66 development in the park was held in April 1960 in the new Rio Grande Village campground. In true Big Bend style, the locally traditional barbeque luncheon followed the ceremony. Pictured below, during the Panther Junction Administration Building dedication in November 1963, officials from the Mexican Department of Parks announce that for the first time since 1936 Mexico would revive work to establish an international park. Mission 66 Advisory Board ex-chairman Frank Masland and National Park Service Director Conrad Wirth were dignitaries attending the Panther Junction Administration Building Dedication. Thirty years earlier, Conrad Wirth was instrumental during the Big Bend Park Project of the 1930s and the major move to establish the international park. (Above, photograph by Harold J. Brodrick; below, photograph by Douglas Evans; both courtesy of National Park Service.)

During the 1950s, the Soil and Moisture Conservation agency made large-scale efforts to reestablish grassland in Tornillo Flat. Overgrazing in the late 1800s and early 1900s had denuded this broad plain, and erosion had become a problem. Above, Otis French drives the tractor-pulled plow and Franciso Franco follows with a shovel to clear brush from the pits where they subsequently planted a variety of grass seeds. In the image below, Bob Gibbs is inspecting range recovery at Todd Hill, northwest of the Chisos. (Above, photograph by Soil and Moisture Conservation Service; below, photograph by Paul Balch and Bob Gibbs; both courtesy of National Park Service.)

In the above photograph, protecting the fragile ecosystem in the Chisos Mountains remains a major focus for park management. This 1950s school brought specialists in fire management into the park to train park employees in proper fire-fighting techniques and safety. Below, protecting park visitors requires park rangers be skilled in technical techniques used in rescues in the rugged backcountry. Training in technical rock climbing and search and rescue have been standard operations from the beginning of the park. (Both courtesy of National Park Service.)

In the early years, park rangers performed a whole host of duties, ranging from interpreting the park's scenery and resources to visitors to cleaning the rest rooms. In this 1957 image, Ranger Naturalist William Bromberg (far left) explains the natural history of the Chisos Mountains to visitors on a nature walk to Juniper Flat. (Photograph by Harold J. Brodrick, courtesy of National Park Service.)

Long-term park employees have always had close ties with neighbors in Mexico, and they found ways to celebrate international friendship. Park employees have individually contributed, in the background, to the health and well-being of neighbors in Mexico. Santa Claus Emory Lehnert is distributing toys to children in Boquillas, Mexico, at Christmas in 1962. The park attempted to maintain friendly relations with neighbors across the river who also depended on tourism for a substantial part of their livelihood. (Photograph by Douglas Evans, courtesy of National Park Service.)

When disaster struck in the 1958 flood, citizens in Marathon and Alpine sent emergency supplies to the park to aid flood victims in Mexico. Floodwaters isolated Santa Elena, Chihuahua, and park employees and U.S. Customs agents floated supplies across by raft. Record flooding occurred again in both 1978 and 2008, when high water destroyed homes in Ojinaga, Chihuahua, and Presidio, Texas, and damaged farms and ranches on both sides of the Rio Grande for miles downstream. Each of these floods brought extensive assistance from both NPS and others to the flooded Mexican villages. Buildings at Hot Springs have been flooded each of these times during the park's history. (Below, photograph by author; both courtesy of the U.S. National Park Service)

Eight

THESE CAME LATER

During the first quarter century of park history, Big Bend remained relatively obscure. By 1970, marginal ranching potential in southern Brewster County forced several large ranches to sell. Terlingua Ranch was acquired by Great Western Corporation (later becoming Terramar Corporation), a group of speculators from Dallas and Houston.

By this time, the state had already acquired a large tract of land northeast of the national park and established Black Gap Wildlife Management Area. In the 1980s, the state of Texas purchased roughly 250,000 acres and created Big Bend Ranch State Park, the largest state park in Texas.

In the 1970s, Great Western/Terramar subdivided the almost 200,000-acre Terlingua Ranch property into small tracts and reserved several sections for deer hunting. The promise of cheap land and free hunting rights attracted many buyers who purchased land without first seeing it. Most of the land is beautifully rustic, but tracts have no utilities and roads, often no more than a bulldozed track up the side of a mountain, become impassable after a rainstorm. After actually seeing their property, many purchasers sold out to real-estate brokers who capitalized by increasing the land prices.

Terlingua Ranch drew newcomers to Big Bend in unprecedented numbers. Many moved here without truly understanding what it takes to live in such a remote place away from basic necessities and medical care. Once disillusionment set in and the owner sold out, realtors held onto the property until another naive person arrived. On Terlingua Ranch today, the trail of buyers and sellers is visible in the variety of shacks and shanties, modified trailer houses, so-called middle-class homes, diminutive mansions, and a few energy-alternative accommodations, each built according to the dreams of the respective land owners. Undoubtedly, Terlingua Ranch is responsible for the modern growth of south Brewster County.

Some members of the Terlingua Ranch founders are also responsible for starting up the Terlingua World Championship Chili Cook-Off, an event that strikes Big Bend each autumn.

Once called Chiricahua Ranch, the Christmas Mountains dominate the central part of Terlingua Ranch. Both images are from the summit of the Christmas Mountains currently owned by the Texas General Land Office. The above image shows a large portion of Terlingua Ranch in the foreground with Nine Point Mesa and Santiago Mountain in the distance. The below image is of the Terlingua Ranch headquarters that boasts an airstrip, cabins, café, and swimming pool. Recently financial difficulties forced an indefinite shutdown of resort operations. (Both photographs by author.)

To some, Terlingua means the championship chili cook-off. By one account, in 1967, Frank X. Tolbert, who had a knack for tongue-in-cheek humor, and Wick Fowler held the first Terlingua competitive chili fest, somewhat in jest. As beans and green chilis showed up in the concoctions, objections from competitors laid down the rules that only red peppers, coarsely ground meat, and a few other ingredients were allowed—but never with beans. The Chili Appreciation Society International, Inc. holds a chili competition the same weekend as the Wick-Fowler Cook-Off. The popularity of both events spurred similar events elsewhere in the country and in Europe, and a popular restaurant chain was founded on chili dishes. (Both courtesy of Barbara Trammell.)

23rd ANNUAL
ORIGINAL
TERLINGUA INTERNATIONAL
FRANK X. TOLBERT — WICK FOWLER MEMORIAL
CHAMPIONSHIP CHILI COOK-OFF

This year's poster is dedicated to
Hallie Stillwell, Our Chili Queen Since 1967

Photographer,
Tracy Lynch

NOVEMBER 4, 1989
BEHIND THE STORE at VIVA TERLINGUA

Music by GARY P. NUNN — WAYNE KENNEMER
and the "National Band of Texas"

 WOLF CHILI

SPONSORS: WOLF BRAND CHILI • TOLBERT'S CHILI PARLOR
WICK FOWLER'S 2-ALARM CHILI • LONE STAR BEER
SHINER BREWERY • COLONY PARKE HOTEL/DALLAS

During chili cook-off week, the area population grows by about 10,000 souls intent on kicking up their heels. Along with a sudden boost to the local economy come a dozen or more deputies, highway patrolmen, and increased emergency medical aid. Over the years, these events have generated substantial revenue supporting growth of the Terlingua School, fire and emergency medical services, and local businesses. (Courtesy of John Alexander.)

The Chihuahuan Desert Challenge draws several hundred mountain bike enthusiasts from across the nation to a weekend-long rally at Lajitas. Terlingua Medics mobile aid station is commonly present at large events such as this. (Courtesy of John Alexander.)

Nine

THESE ARE HERE TODAY

In the 1970s, the Rio Grande Guides Association began promoting river rafting and canoeing. At first, Glen Pepper ran an outfitting business from Villa de la Mina, west of Terlingua Ghostown. About 1978, Far Flung Adventures set up their world headquarters in Terlingua Ghostown. At one time, around a half-dozen river outfitters provided year-round service, but today less than a handful of local outfitters provide such services.

A few stores provided for local residents in the 1970s. Northeast of the park was Hallie Stillwell's store. The Study Butte Store, Rex Ivey's Lajitas Trading Post, and Paul "Terlingua" Vonn's store in the Ghostown served the west side of the park. National Parks Concessions, Inc. operated stores at the developed areas inside the park. These commercial enterprises comprised the closest sources of groceries and dry goods south of U.S. Highway 90 and supplied the basic beans, beer, and gasoline.

Lajitas experienced a most dramatic face alteration in the late 1970s when Walter Mischer constructed a quaint western-style boardwalk and hotel dominated by an authentic saloon (popular with the locals). His nine-hole golf course in the Rio Grande floodplain, however, was frequently flooded. Mischer sold out to entrepreneur Steve Smith, who poured millions into the resort, expanding the golf course to 18 holes. Lajitas Trading Post, a thriving business prior to Smith's acquisition, was forced to close due to financial problems. Finances finally forced Smith to sell out to the highest bidder who, shortly after acquiring the property, watched the golf course disappear under the 2008 Rio Grande flood.

If a postscript applies somewhere in the evolution of Big Bend, perhaps it should simply state that as elsewhere in the universe, the face of the place changes constantly. The desert is self-limiting—people are limited by the natural processes at work here. If a person does not like the weather, wait 15 minutes. The sun's light, shifting across the rugged surface of this magnificent land, constantly repaints the scene with surreal magic. Sit quietly and watch, and it will fill the soul with awe.

Visitors to the Chisos Basin today find an array of more modern buildings. The Basin Ranger Station–Visitor Center and the Chisos Basin Store were built in the late 1980s to replace earlier structures. The Chisos Lodge motel units built by National Parks Concessions, Inc. in the 1960s are still in use, as well as three two-story ranch style units, built at the same time as the new store and ranger station. (Both photographs by author.)

Far Flung Adventures, operating from Terlingua Ghostown, ran occasional river trips in Mexico. Two of the founders of Far Flung Adventures pictured here are Mike Davidson (far left) and Steve Harris (far right) with their Mexican guides while scouting the Rio Grande de Santiago in Jalisco for possible commercial river trips. (Courtesy of John Morlock.)

Lower Canyons is an approximately 90-mile stretch of the Rio Grande Wild and Scenic River. Here the Rio Grande passes through some of the most isolated and inhospitable country in North America. The moist river corridor is closely confined within the narrow walls of spectacular desert terrain. In the raft are Tommy Conners (left) and Malcolm MacRoberts, and in the kayak is Steve Belardo, running Lower Canyons in 1981. (Courtesy of John Morlock.)

High water can turn otherwise sluggish flows into raging torrents that challenge novices and white-water masters alike. (Courtesy of John Morlock.)

Pictured above is Black George Simmons, a retired veteran from the U.S. Geological Survey who has literally traversed the highlands of Tibet to the jungles of Amazon. Simmons is responsible for naming several geologic features in the Grand Canyon. He is seen here on a tequila smugglers trail near Complejo del Caballo in the Lower Canyons. This hand-laid trail was well used during Prohibition. Below, rocky rapids are difficult to traverse when shallow, requiring boaters to hand-line canoes and rafts through tight squeezes. A careless move during such an event can quickly pin a canoe against the rocks where the seemingly slow current empirically demonstrates its amazing power, making extraction impossible without use of technical gear to dislodge the craft. (Courtesy of John Morlock.)

A famous obstacle on the Rio Grande is the Rockslide Rapid in Santa Elena Canyon. The Puppy Nose is a landmark used to identify the appropriate channel to take through the Rockslide at low water but should be avoided at high water levels. (Photograph by Anne Bellamy, courtesy of John Morlock.)

The heat of the desert summers makes river running a seasonal business. This forced several river companies to shut down operations and leave their abandoned buildings behind. Occasionally restaurants or curio shops reoccupied such buildings. (Photograph by author.)

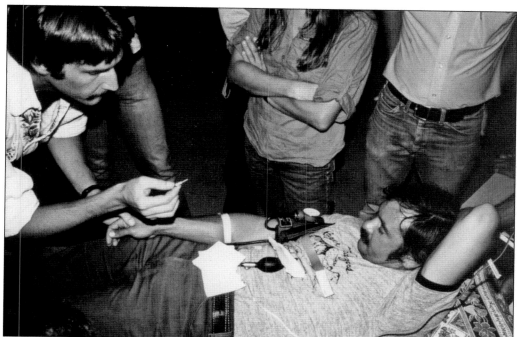

Pictured above is John Alexander, son of a prominent doctor in Denver, who is primarily responsible for the establishment and early growth of emergency services in south Brewster County. The vastness of south Brewster County requires cooperation between the park and local communities to provide emergency fire and medical services. Terlingua Medics provided all levels of first-aid training to many volunteers. In this photograph, John Alexander demonstrates insertion of an intravenous fluid system on park ranger George Howarth. The mountainous terrain of Big Bend creates problems for radio communications, and John Alexander was also instrumental in establishing radio repeaters at critical locations that provided maximum coverage for the south Brewster County service area. Shown at right atop Christmas Mountains, John tests radio reception for several agencies' frequencies. (Both courtesy of John Alexander and Terlingua Fire and Emergency Services.)

Big Bend has provided background scenery for several movies including *Fandango*, *Uphill All The Way*, *Streets of Laredo*, and *Spy Kids II* among others. In the above image, the author offers a toast to the "DOM" rock from *Fandango* (1985), starring Kevin Costner. Below, in this 1985 filming of *Uphill All The Way*, several locals work as part of the cast. Standing in the center to the left of Glen Campbell (with beard) is Terry Davidson, and Jim Burr is standing on the right; standing on the left, aiming the rifle, is an unidentified production company employee; crouched at the lower left are Jack Defoe and Richard Sharpe; the person in white, behind the car, is Burl Ives. This photograph was shot at the *Contrabando* movie set on Big Bend Ranch State Park, west of Lajitas. (Above, photograph by Betty Alex; below, photograph by John Alexander.)

The 1980 census revealed that south Brewster County had a higher per capita education than most of the country. Ample shade and cold beer attracted boatmen, desert rats, a Ph.D. physicist, and assorted escapees from urbanity who engaged in metaphysical discussions that could fill volumes of social commentaries. Study Butte Store remains an oasis supplying fuel and food, sponsoring Fourth of July fireworks and parade, and hosting egg hunting at Easter. The local hangout has migrated to the Ghostown, where "Doctor" Doug Blackmon, one of the more enlightened persons there, is often seen standing on the porch in front of Terlingua Trading Company (at right). The infusion of psychoactive liquids undoubtedly spurs the swapping of lore and lies. When someone shows up with a guitar, it fuels a chorus of melodies long into the night. (Above, photograph by author; at right, photograph by Carolyn Burr.)

Behind the modern scene lies an ethereal image of miners and their families walking into the Perry Store (now Terlingua Trading Company), the ice cream parlor (currently an artist gallery), and the movie theater (now the Starlight Theater Restaurant). From this porch, the sunset view to the east is often more spectacular than it is to the west. (Photograph by author.)

This tumbling-down ruin was a classroom to the children of miners at Study Butte. This ruin, like most others scattered across the Big Bend landscape, still holds the essence of those who filled its spaces in the past. (Photograph by author.)

In Study Butte, Uncle Joe's burgers were once a major attraction, followed by Aunt Roberta's café, Boatman's Bar and Grill, Ms. Tracie's café, and now El Centro's collectibles shop and bottled water supplier. (Photograph by author.)

Many evenings were spent indulging in pizza, Mexican food, and cerveza at Pancho's Restaurant, now the educational extension of the Baptist church. (Photograph by author.)

Much of Big Bend's physical history lies in ruins or has vanished into the desert, but its oral tradition survives in the descendants of those early pioneers. Today people who value the nation's heritage work together to capture those living historical remnants of the fleeting past before it is obscured by the present. Pictured here in the first row on the steps of the Ghostown theater are, from left to right, J. Travis Roberts, chairman of the Brewster County Historical Commission; and Melissa Keane, historical archeologist for the Center for Big Bend Studies. Sitting in the second row from left to right are Thomas Alex, archeologist for Big Bend National Park; Cynta de Narvaez, Ghostown historian; and Tim Roberts, West Texas cultural resources coordinator for Texas Parks and Wildlife Department. (Photograph by Sandra Rogers.)

Until the border closure in 2002, the Rio Grande's moist corridor joined the arid lands along its two shores. The canyons provided thrilling and challenging recreation, villages in Mexico provided places for park visitors to experience the relaxed atmosphere of rural Mexico, and the Mexican people depended on the amenities that are easier to reach on the U.S. side than in their remote frontier. Here in Big Bend, the river joined two nations rather than dividing them. Perhaps, one day, enlightenment will rise once more and there will finally be an international peace park at Big Bend. (Photograph W. Ray Scott, courtesy National Parks Concessions, Inc.)

DISCOVER THOUSANDS OF LOCAL HISTORY BOOKS FEATURING MILLIONS OF VINTAGE IMAGES

Arcadia Publishing, the leading local history publisher in the United States, is committed to making history accessible and meaningful through publishing books that celebrate and preserve the heritage of America's people and places.

Find more books like this at
www.arcadiapublishing.com

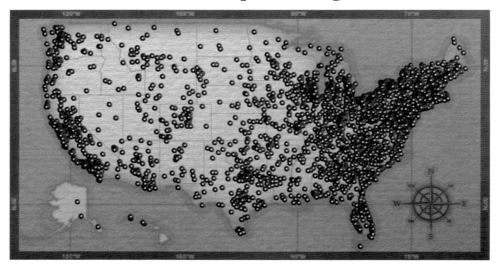

Search for your hometown history, your old stomping grounds, and even your favorite sports team.